AARDVARKS

Emma Bassier

DiscoverRoo
An Imprint of Pop!
popbooksonline.com

abdobooks.com

Published by Pop!, a division of ABDO, PO Box 398166, Minneapolis, Minnesota 55439. Copyright © 2020 by POP, LLC. International copyrights reserved in all countries. No part of this book may be reproduced in any form without written permission from the publisher. Pop!™ is a trademark and logo of POP, LLC.

Printed in the United States of America, North Mankato, Minnesota.

102019
012020

Cover Photo: Shutterstock Images
Interior Photos: Shutterstock Images, 1, 4–5, 8, 13, 20, 29, 30, 31; iStockphoto, 6, 15, 16–17, 19; Red Line Editorial, 7; Nigel Dennis/Newscom, 9; Josef Vostarek/CTK/AP Images, 11; Kaoru Tachibana/The Yomiuri Shimbun/AP Images, 12; Frank Rumpenhorst/picture–alliance/dpa/AP Images, 14; Zjan/Supplied by Wenn.com/Newscom, 16; Nigel J Dennis/NHPA/Photoshot/Newscom, 17 (top); Martin Harvey/Alamy, 17 (middle); Images of Africa Photobank/Alamy, 21; Philip Perry/

FLPA imageBroker/Newscom, 22; Nigel Dennis imageBroker/Newscom, 23, 25; Alessandra Pezzotta/Alamy, 26–27; H. Schmidbauer/picture alliance/blickwinkel/H/Newscom, 28

Editor: Nick Rebman
Series Designer: Jake Slavik

Library of Congress Control Number: 2019942477

Publisher's Cataloging-in-Publication Data

Names: Bassier, Emma, author.
Title: Aardvarks / by Emma Bassier
Description: Minneapolis, Minnesota : Pop!, 2020 | Series: Weird and wonderful animals | Includes online resources and index.
Identifiers: ISBN 9781532166013 (lib. bdg.) | ISBN 9781644943311 (pbk.) | ISBN 9781532167331 (ebook)
Subjects: LCSH: Aardvark--Juvenile literature. | Ant bear--Juvenile literature. | Oddities--Juvenile literature. | Insect-eating animals--Juvenile literature. | Nocturnal animals--Juvenile literature.
Classification: DDC 599.314--dc23

WELCOME TO
DiscoverRoo!

Pop open this book and you'll find QR codes loaded with information, so you can learn even more!

Scan this code* and others like it while you read, or visit the website below to make this book pop!

popbooksonline.com/aardvarks

*Scanning QR codes requires a web-enabled smart device with a QR code reader app and a camera.

TABLE OF
CONTENTS

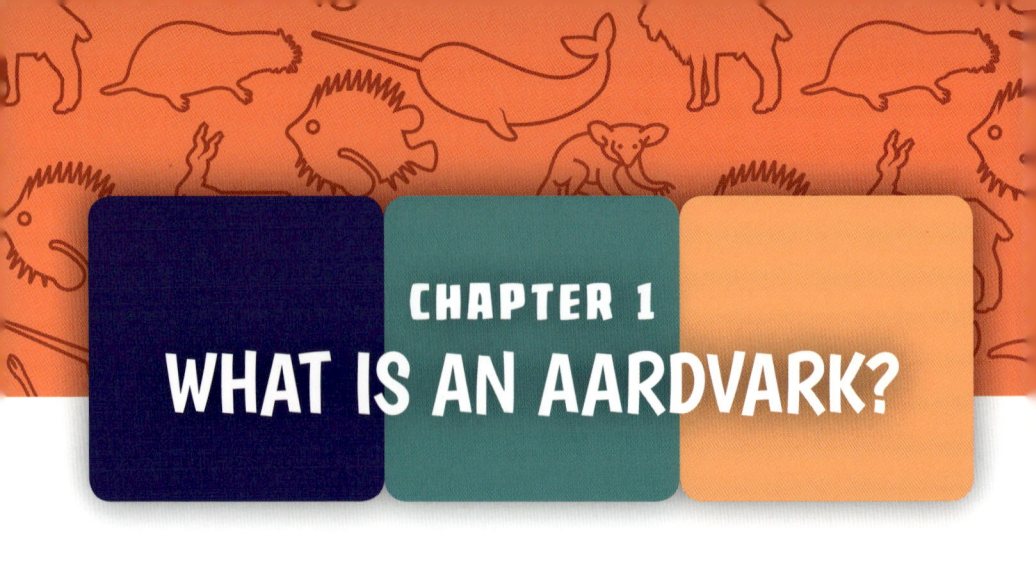

CHAPTER 1
WHAT IS AN AARDVARK?

A hairy animal crawls out of its **burrow** after sunset. The creature's long ears look like a rabbit's. But its

WATCH A VIDEO HERE!

nose is similar to a pig snout. And its stiff tail is like a kangaroo's. This is not an imaginary creature. It is an aardvark!

Aardvarks roam the plains of Africa.

Aardvarks are **mammals** that live in Africa. Many aardvarks live in woodlands and rain forests. These **habitats** have trees and soft soil. Aardvarks also live in savannas. Savannas are grasslands with scattered trees.

DID YOU KNOW? The word *aardvark* comes from an Afrikaans word meaning "earth pig."

RANGE MAP

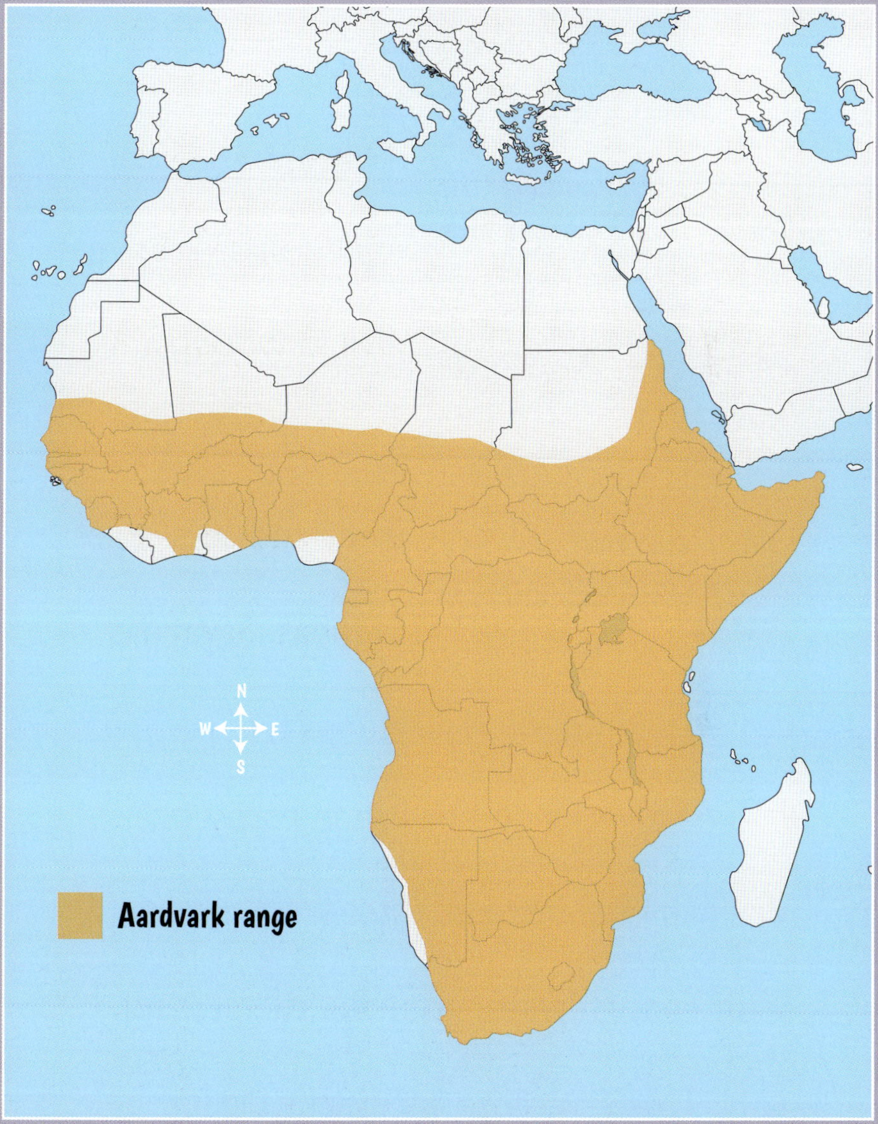

Aardvark range

Savannas are common in many parts of central and southern Africa.

Aardvarks do not live in rocky or dry habitats. Instead, they live in places with enough water to make the ground soft. That's because aardvarks dig

burrows in the ground. Sand and loose

dirt are easier for them to dig into.

DID YOU KNOW?

Aardvarks can live for more than 20 years.

An aardvark digs into the ground to create a burrow.

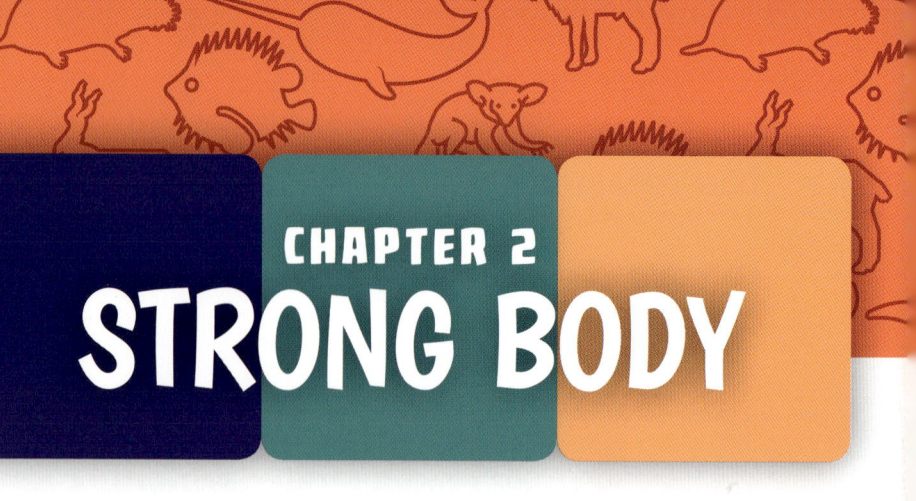

CHAPTER 2
STRONG BODY

An aardvark is the same size as a large dog. It can weigh between 110 and 180 pounds (50–82 kg). An aardvark has thick skin. Its body is covered in thin hairs.

COMPLETE AN ACTIVITY HERE!

A zookeeper spends time with an aardvark.

An adult aardvark is usually

64 to 79 inches (163–201 cm) long.

Approximately one-third of that length

is the animal's tail.

An aardvark displays its long, pink tongue.

An aardvark has a long tongue. The tongue can be more than 10 inches (25 cm) in length. An aardvark's snout

sticks out from its face. The snout has

ten bones in it. These bones help the

animal pick up scents.

An aardvark walks through the sand, using its powerful nose to search for food.

A young aardvark shows off its nails.

Aardvarks have powerful legs. Their front legs have four toes. The back legs have five toes. Each toe has a tough, flat nail. These nails are like a combination of hooves and claws.

DID YOU KNOW?

Most of the time, aardvarks do not chew their food. Instead, their strong stomach muscles break down food.

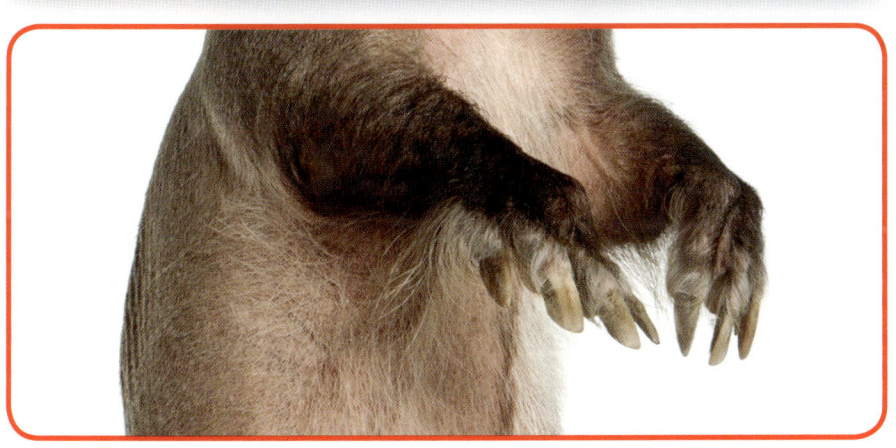

LIFE CYCLE OF AN AARDVARK

The calf lives with its mother for approximately six months.

A female aardvark gives birth to one baby, or calf, each year.

Then the calf moves out and digs its own **burrow**.

Aardvarks live on their own.

They come together only for mating.

CHAPTER 3
HUNGRY INVADER

Aardvarks eat ants and termites. They need to eat lots of insects to fuel their large bodies. An aardvark's strong senses of smell and hearing help it find food.

When an aardvark finds an insect mound, it scrapes the mound with its

LEARN MORE HERE!

Ants make up a major part of an aardvark's diet.

sharp nails. Then the aardvark breaks the

mound open. When that happens, the

insects crawl to the surface.

An aardvark uses its long, sticky tongue to suck up insects from the mound. While eating, the aardvark closes its nostrils. This keeps dust and insects out of its nose.

An aardvark keeps its nose low to the ground while searching for food.

An aardvark sticks its head into an insect nest to find a meal.

Angry ants and termites may try to bite an aardvark that **invades** their home. But the aardvark's thick skin protects it from painful bites.

DID YOU KNOW?

Termite mounds can be as hard as cement.

An aardvark digs a burrow in the dirt.

An aardvark uses its nails and strong

legs to dig **burrows** in the ground.

Aardvarks are some of the fastest diggers in Africa. This makes it easy for them to move locations.

BURYING POOP

Aardvarks bury their poop. They cover it with dirt. Scientists think they do this to hide the smell of the termites they ate. The aardvarks don't want other insects to detect this smell and leave the area.

An aardvark emerges from its burrow.

CHAPTER 4
NIGHT LIFE

Aardvarks are nocturnal. That means they are most active at night. During the night, an aardvark leaves its **burrow** to find food. The aardvark may travel several miles each night.

Aardvarks have poor eyesight. Instead, they rely on smelling and hearing to learn about their surroundings.

An aardvark searches for food.

LEARN MORE HERE!

Aardvarks spend a lot of time sniffing the ground and listening.

DID YOU KNOW? Ants and termites are nocturnal, just like aardvarks.

During the day, an aardvark stays

in its burrow. An aardvark burrow

can be up to 10 feet (3.0 m) deep. The

burrow shades the aardvark from the

An aardvark rests in its burrow.

sun. It also gives the animal a safe place

to sleep. **Predators** such as lions and

hyenas hunt aardvarks. But they can't get

aardvarks in their burrows.

An aardvark walks alone in search of a meal.

Aardvarks do not live in groups.

Living alone can be helpful for finding

enough food to eat. That way, an

aardvark doesn't have to share its food.

DID YOU KNOW?

Some aardvarks dig new burrows each day instead of going back to old ones.

An aardvark digs a burrow in the African country of Namibia.

MAKING CONNECTIONS

TEXT-TO-SELF

Would you want to see an aardvark up close? Why or why not?

TEXT-TO-TEXT

Have you read another book about an animal that lives in a burrow? How is that animal similar to or different from an aardvark?

TEXT-TO-WORLD

Aardvarks rely on their senses of smell and hearing to get around. What would life be like if you used only your nose and ears to learn about your surroundings?

GLOSSARY

burrow – a hole that an animal digs in the ground.

habitat – the area where an animal normally lives.

invade – to enter and take over an area by force.

mammal – a type of animal that has hair or fur and feeds milk to its young.

predator – an animal that hunts other animals for food.

INDEX

ONLINE RESOURCES
popbooksonline.com

Scan this code* and others like it while you read, or visit the website below to make this book pop!

popbooksonline.com/aardvarks

*Scanning QR codes requires a web-enabled smart device with a QR code reader app and a camera.